READY for Learning World
WORKBOOK

pink
red
orange
yellow
green
blue
purple
brown
black
gray
white

JN122193

two 2 2

four 4 4

eight 8 8

one 1 1

nine 9 9

six 6 6

three 3 3

five 5 5

ten 10 10

seven 7 7

A B C D E F G H I J K L M N O P Q R S T U V W X Y Z

Lower case

a

b

c

d

e

f

g

h

i

j

k

l

m

n

o

p

q

r

s

t

u

v

w

x

y

z

Upper case

書きじゅんに決まりはありません。この書きじゅんは 1 つのれいです。

Let's color.

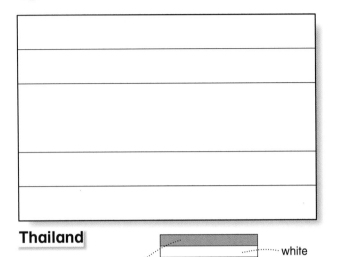

Thailand

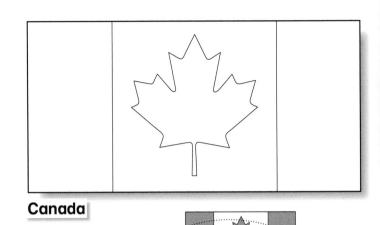

Canada

red ······ white ······ blue ······ white

red ······ white

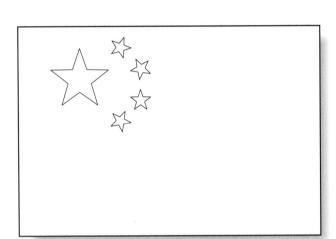

China

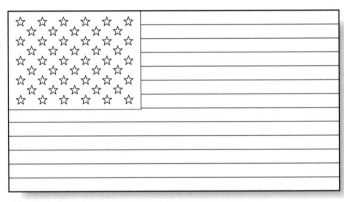

U.S.A.

yellow ······ red

white ······ red
blue ······ white

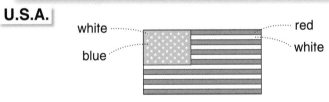

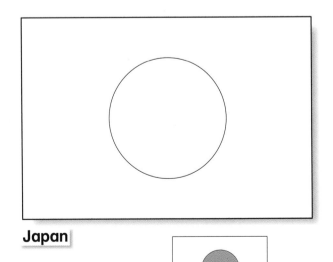

Japan

Mexico

white ······ red

brown ······ red
green ······ white

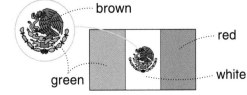

What can you see?

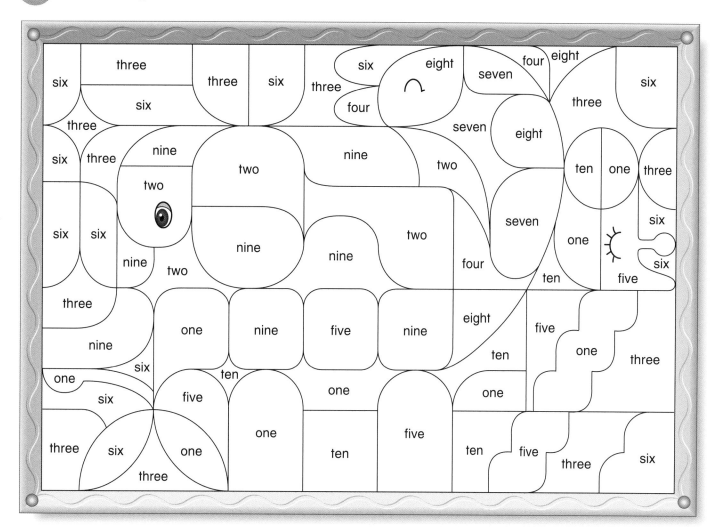

Color key

pink	green	blue	yellow
3 + 3 = ☐	3 + 6 = ☐	2 + 5 = ☐	3 + 2 = ☐
9 − 3 = ☐	2 + 7 = ☐	7 × 1 = ☐	8 − 3 = ☐
8 − 5 = ☐	9 − 7 = ☐	9 − 5 = ☐	0 + 1 = ☐
2 × 3 = ☐	3 × 3 = ☐	2 × 4 = ☐	2 × 5 = ☐
5 − 2 = ☐	2 × 1 = ☐	6 − 2 = ☐	8 + 2 = ☐
4 + 2 = ☐	7 − 5 = ☐	7 + 1 = ☐	1 × 1 = ☐
3 × 1 = ☐	5 + 4 = ☐	2 × 2 = ☐	5 − 4 = ☐

Complete the Color key before coloring the picture above.
まず、カラーキーを計算して見つけてから上の絵をぬりましょう。

Let's color.

1 three blue cats

2 two green cats

3 five orange cats

4 one brown cat

5 seven black cats

6 six red cats

7 four pink cats

8 eight yellow cats

9 nine white cats

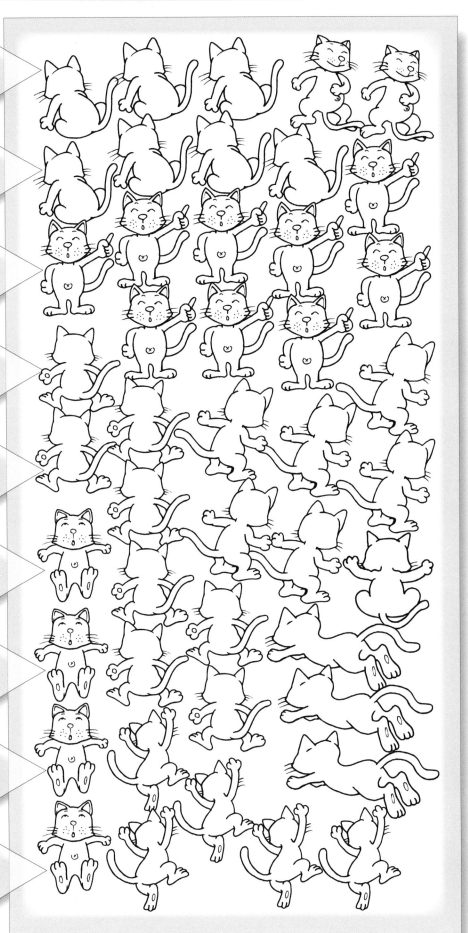

→ Refer to p.1.

Let's write!

四線からはみ出さないように、ていねいにね。①から⑧はカタカナでよく使っている「身につけるもの」の単語だよ。

① bag

② cap

③ pants

④ shirt

⑤ shoes

⑥ skirt

⑦ sneakers

⑧ sweater

⑨ bike

⑩ flag

⑪ school

⑫ school bus

⑬ cloud

⑭ flower

⑮ sun

⑯ tree

Let's write.

What are you wearing today?

I am wearing a shirt,

What are you wearing today?

I am wearing

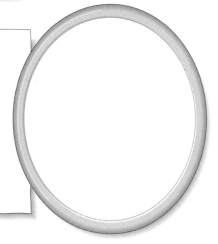

How do you come to school?

I come to school

by bus   by bike   by train   by car   on foot

A B C D E F G H I J K L M N O P Q R S T U V W X Y Z

A	d
B	a
C	e
D	b
E	c
F	f

S	x
T	u
U	t
V	s
W	v
X	w

G	h
H	g
I	k
J	l
K	i
L	j

Y	i
Z	d
D	y
B	n
I	b
N	z

M	r
N	n
O	o
P	p
Q	m
R	q

M	o
O	m
Q	q
E	t
T	s
S	e

A

This is my friend.

His name is Robert.

He is ten years old.

1 What is his name?

_____

_____

_____

2 How old is he?

_____

_____

_____

B

This is my friend.

Her name is Cathy.

She is nine years old.

1 What is her name?

_____

_____

_____

2 How old is she?

_____

_____

_____

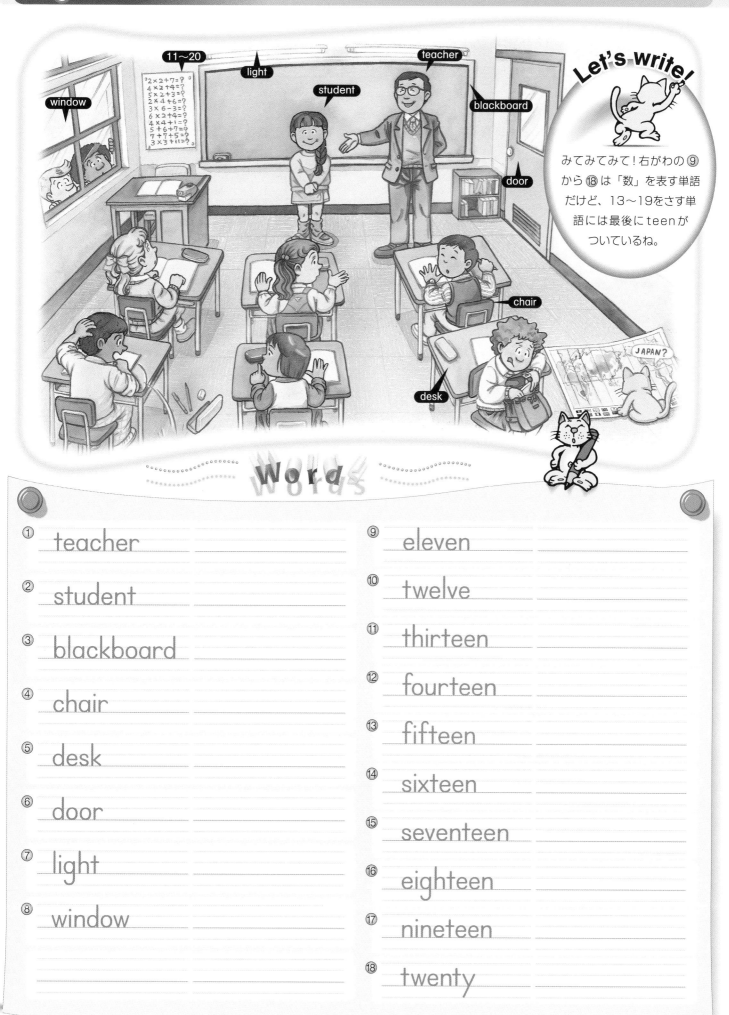

Let's write!

みてみてみて！右がわの⑨から⑱は「数」を表す単語だけど、13～19をさす単語には最後にteenがついているね。

~~~~~~~~~ **Words** ~~~~~~~~~

① teacher

② student

③ blackboard

④ chair

⑤ desk

⑥ door

⑦ light

⑧ window

⑨ eleven

⑩ twelve

⑪ thirteen

⑫ fourteen

⑬ fifteen

⑭ sixteen

⑮ seventeen

⑯ eighteen

⑰ nineteen

⑱ twenty

What time is it?

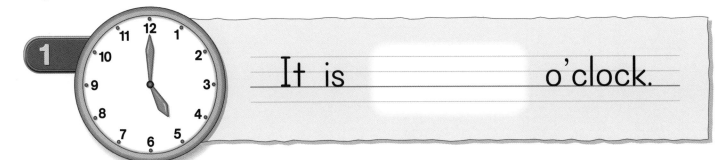

1 It is _____ o'clock.

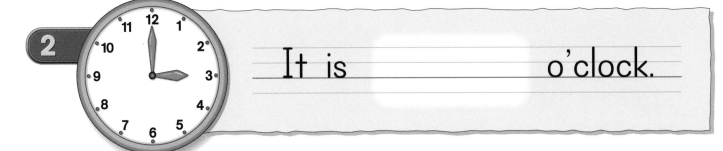

2 It is _____ o'clock.

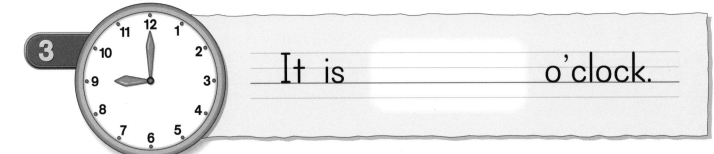

3 It is _____ o'clock.

4 It is _____ o'clock.

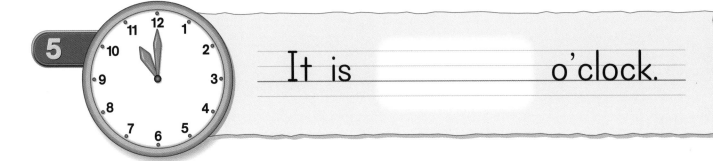

5 It is _____ o'clock.

1	2	3	4	5	6	7	8	9	10	11	12
one	two	three	four	five	six	seven	eight	nine	ten	eleven	twelve

A B C D E F G H I J K L M N O P Q R S T U V W X Y Z

Upper case	Lower case
TREE	tree
1 CAT	
2 DESK	
3	school
4	friends
5 STUDENT	
6	window
7 TEACHER	

13

Write the days in order.

Monday, Friday, Thursday, Saturday, Sunday, Tuesday, Wednesday

1

What's this in English?

It is _____ in English.

2

What's this in English?

3

What's this in English?

4

What's this in English?

Encourage students to find the words in their textbooks.
テキストのなかで単語のつづりを見つけるように指導しましょう。

① chalk

② eraser

③ pencil

④ pencil case

⑤ ruler

⑥ scissors

⑦ stapler

⑧ textbook

⑨ English

⑩ Japanese

⑪ math

⑫ music

⑬ P.E.

⑭ science

⑮ social studies

⑯ Life Environment Studies

Choose the right answer.

1

Is this a ruler?

Yes, it is.
No, it isn't.

2

Is this a pencil case?

Yes, it is.
No, it isn't.

3

Is this an eraser?

Yes, it is.
No, it isn't.

4

Is this a pencil?

Yes, it is.
No, it isn't.

5

Is this a ruler?

Yes, it is.
No, it isn't.

What is the first letter? A B C D E F G H I J K L M N O P Q R S T U V W X Y Z

a — red   b — blue   c — yellow   d — green

Hopscotch

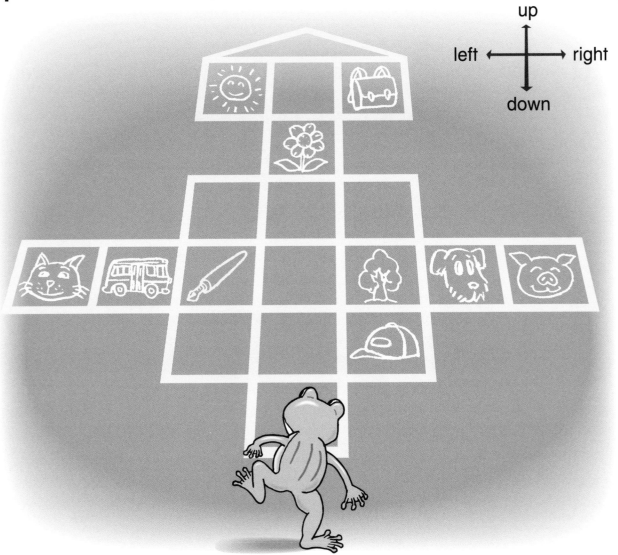

1 Hop **three** blocks **up** and **three** blocks **left**.

What do you see?

2 Hop **four** blocks **up**, **one** block **right** and **two** blocks **down**.

What do you see?

3 Hop **six** blocks **up** and **one** block **right**.

What do you see?

Let's write!

「てつぼう」って何ていうんだっけ？ horizon は「水平」っていう意味だよ。 climb の さいごのbは、読まない 字だよ！

Words

① run

② climb

③ kick

④ catch

⑤ throw

⑥ jungle gym

⑦ slide

⑧ swing

⑨ horizontal bar

⑩ monkey bars

⑪ baseball

⑫ basketball

⑬ dodgeball

⑭ soccer

⑮ volleyball

Yes, let's.   No, let's not.

●soccer

●basketball

● Let's play soccer!

No, let's not.

❶ Let's play dodgeball!

●run

❷ Let's play baseball!

●baseball

❸ Let's walk!

❹ Let's play volleyball!

●dodgeball

●swim

❺ Let's run!

❻ Let's play basketball!

●walk

●volleyball

❼ Let's swim!

Initial Letters

A B C D E F G H I J K L M N O P Q R S T U V W X Y Z

1. _____ ish

2. _____ ear

3. _____ gg

4. _____ at

5. _____ og

6. _____ ouse

7. _____ pple

8. _____ ragon

9. _____ us

10. _____ orilla

11. _____ inger

12. _____ lass

Read each word slowly, emphasizing the sound of the initial letter.

is   isn't

1 She _____ sad.

2 _____ angry.

3 _____ happy.

she

he

it

Draw your face.

I

Draw a face in each box and complete the sentences.

1 I am _____

2 I am _____

3 I am _____

happy

sad

tired

brave

hungry

Let's write!

「ナイフ」は一番最初に発音しないkがつくから要注意。「スパゲッティー」もなかなか手ごわいぞ。

① apple		⑨ spaghetti	
② fried chicken		⑩ fork	
③ hamburger		⑪ glass	
④ milk		⑫ knife	
⑤ orange juice		⑬ plate	
⑥ pizza		⑭ spoon	
⑦ salad		⑮ table	
⑧ sandwich		⑯ tray	

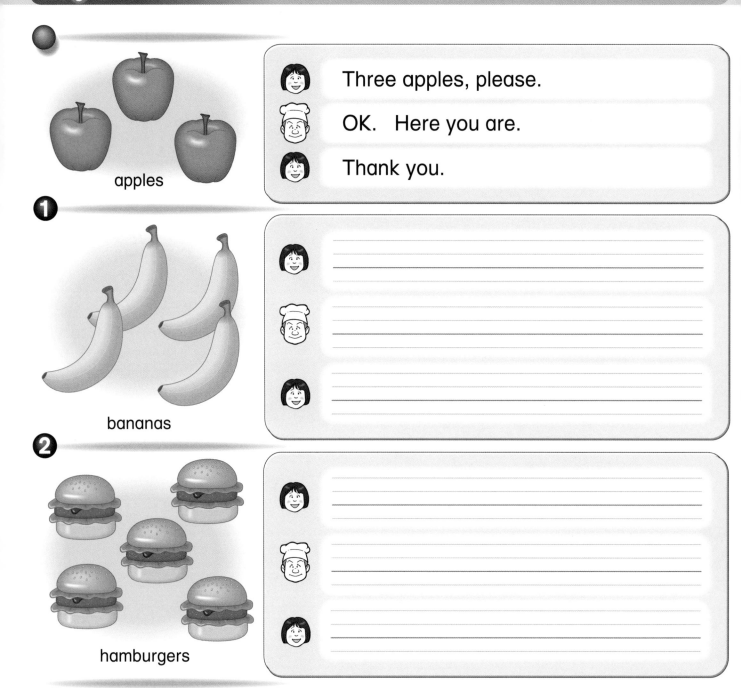

apples

Three apples, please.

OK.　Here you are.

Thank you.

1

bananas

2

hamburgers

The Dish Knights

1 How many spoons?

2 How many forks?

3 How many plates?

A B C D E F G H I J K L M N O P Q R S T U V W X Y Z

F f

1

2

3

4

5

6

7

A　Yes, I can.　No, I can't.

1 Can you swim?

2 Can you cook?

3 Can you catch a frog?

4 Can you play the piano?

5 Can you ride a unicycle?

swim

catch a frog

ride a unicycle

play the piano

cook

B　can　can't

1 I _____ swim.

2 I _____ cook.

3 I _____ catch a frog.

4 I _____ play the piano.

5 I _____ ride a unicycle.

Let's write!

「うで」と「ゆび」と「手」と「足」
はひとつじゃないから、単語
の最後に s がつくんだよ。
20から90までの数は
ty でおわってるね。

① arms

② chin

③ face

④ feet

⑤ fingers

⑥ hair

⑦ hands

⑧ legs

⑨ teeth

⑩ twenty

⑪ thirty

⑫ forty

⑬ fifty

⑭ sixty

⑮ seventy

⑯ eighty

⑰ ninety

⑱ one hundred

27

I am a dinosaur.
I am big. I am tall.
I am six meters tall.
I weigh 2000kg.

1 What are you?   I am a _____.

2 How tall are you?   I am _____.

3 How much do you weigh?   I weigh _____.

What can you do?

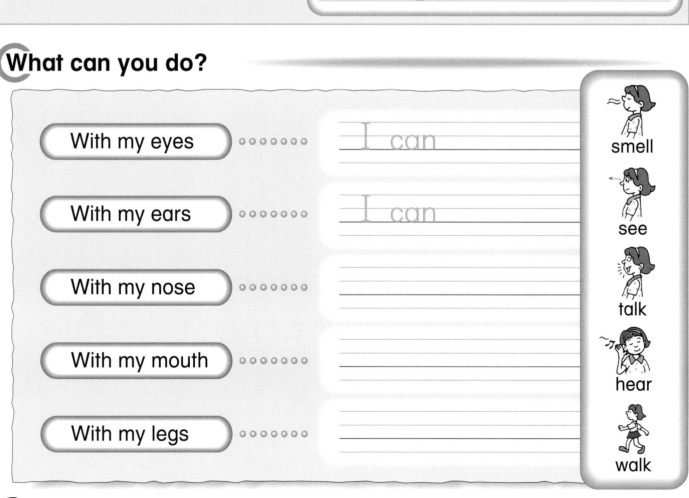

With my eyes   ● ● ● ● ● ● ●   I can _____   smell

With my ears   ● ● ● ● ● ● ●   I can _____   see

With my nose   ● ● ● ● ● ● ●   _____   talk

With my mouth ● ● ● ● ● ● ●   _____   hear

With my legs   ● ● ● ● ● ● ●   _____   walk

What is the first letter?

o — yellow   h — green   p — black   n — red   g — pink   m — blue

How is the weather today?

It is _____ today.

Circle the answer.

1	Is it sunny today?	Yes, it is.	No, it isn't.
2	Is it rainy today?	Yes, it is.	No, it isn't.
3	Is it windy today?	Yes, it is.	No, it isn't.
4	Is it snowy today?	Yes, it is.	No, it isn't.
5	Is it cloudy today?	Yes, it is.	No, it isn't.
6	Is it hot today?	Yes, it is.	No, it isn't.
7	Is it cold today?	Yes, it is.	No, it isn't.

sunny

rainy

windy

snowy

cloudy

hot

cold

is   isn't

1 It _____ sunny today.

2 It _____ cloudy today.

3 It _____ hot today.

Let's write!

へぇー。「ピーマン」は、英語では『ピーマン』って書かないんだ。「とんぼ」は『とんでるドラゴン』って書くんだね。

bird
corn
spider
caterpillar
carrot
little / big
pumpkin
potato
ant
dragonfly
cabbage
lettuce
tomato
green pepper
onion
cucumber
grasshopper

Words

① cabbage
② carrot
③ cucumber
④ corn
⑤ green pepper
⑥ lettuce
⑦ onion
⑧ potato
⑨ pumpkin
⑩ tomato
⑪ little/big
⑫ ant
⑬ dragonfly
⑭ caterpillar
⑮ bird
⑯ grasshopper
⑰ spider

like   don't like

1 I _____ cabbage.

2 I _____ onions.

3 I _____ pumpkins.

4 I _____ carrots.

5 I _____ spiders.

6 I _____ grasshoppers.

Look and answer.

Sunday	Monday	Tuesday	Wednesday	Thursday	Friday	Saturday
	1 ☀	2 ☀	3 ☁	4 ☔	5 ☔	6 ☀
7 ☁	8 ☀	9 ☁	10 ☁	11 ☔	12 ☁	13 ☀
14 ☀	15 ☀	16 ☁	17 ☀	18 ☁	19 ☀	20 ☁
21 ☔	22 ☔	23 ☁	24 ☀	25 ☀	26 ☁	27 ☀
28 ☀	29 ☁	30 ☀				

1 How many sunny days? _____

2 How many rainy days? _____

3 How many cloudy days? _____

10 ten	11 eleven	12 twelve	13 thirteen	14 fourteen	15 fifteen	16 sixteen	17 seventeen	18 eighteen	19 nineteen	20 twenty

Initial Letters

A B C D E F G H I J K L M N O P Q R S T U V W X Y Z

1 ___ ree

7 ___ omato

2 ___ un

8 ___ arrot

3 ___ ing

9 ___ pider

4 ___ abbit

10 ___ onkey

5 ___ ird

11 ___ range

6 ___ nt

12 ___ ajamas

Read each word slowly, emphasizing the sound of the initial letter.

1

Where is your mother?

She is in the

2

Where is your father?

He is

3

Where is your grandpa?

He

4

Where is your grandma?

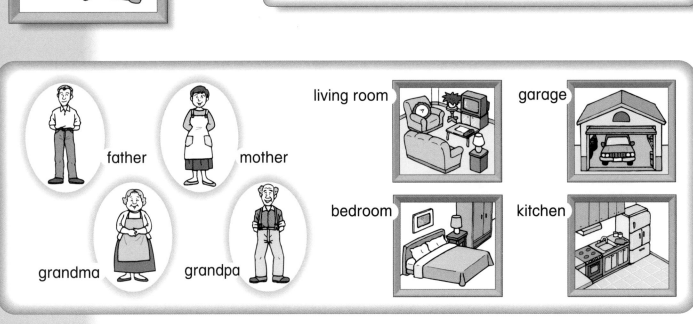

father

mother

grandma

grandpa

living room

garage

bedroom

kitchen

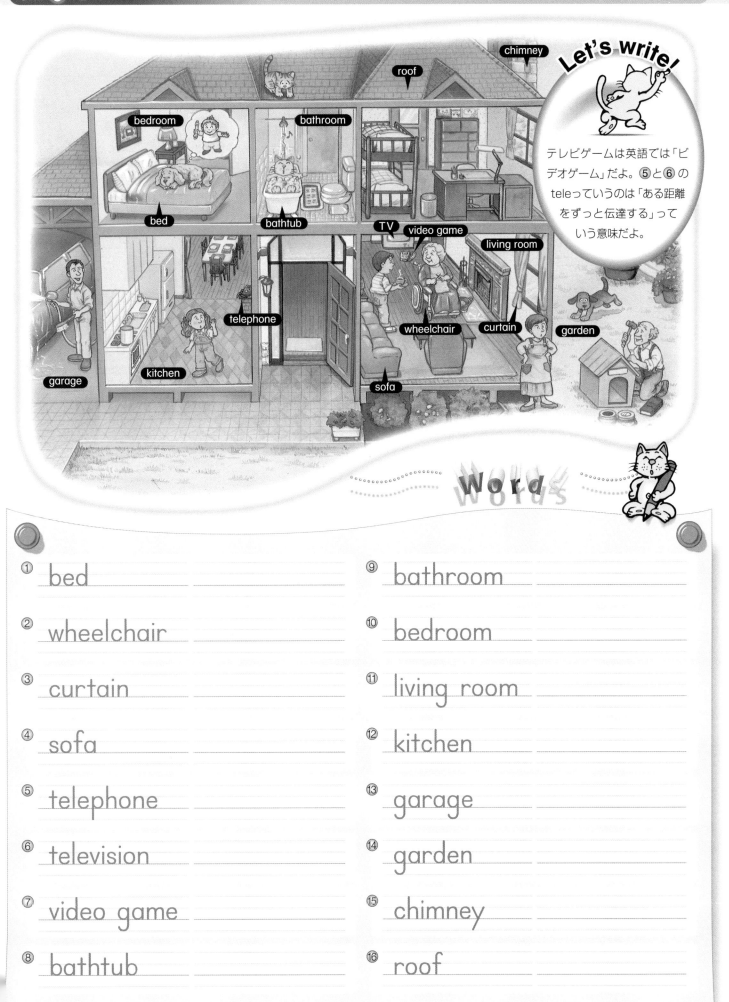

Let's write!

テレビゲームは英語では「ビデオゲーム」だよ。⑤と⑥のteleっていうのは「ある距離をずっと伝達する」っていう意味だよ。

Words

①	bed	⑨	bathroom
②	wheelchair	⑩	bedroom
③	curtain	⑪	living room
④	sofa	⑫	kitchen
⑤	telephone	⑬	garage
⑥	television	⑭	garden
⑦	video game	⑮	chimney
⑧	bathtub	⑯	roof

C What is he doing?

1

What is he doing?

He is

2

What is she doing?

3

What is he doing?

4

What is he doing?

5

What is it doing?

It is

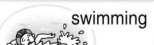 swimming   flying   running   climbing

walking   hopping   skipping   dancing

Let's find words starting with each letter.

A a _____

B b _____

C c _____

D d _____

E e _____

F f _____

G g _____

H h _____

I i _____

J j _____

K k _____

L l _____

M m _____

Encourage students to find words that start with each letter in their textbooks.
Pronounce each word.

A Put the months in order.

March
May
January
November
June
February
April
July
September
December
October
August

_____
_____
March
_____
_____
_____
_____
_____
_____
_____
_____

B Answer the questions.

1 What is the first month?

_____

2 What is the second month?

_____

3 What is the fourth month?

_____

4 What is the tenth month?

_____

5 What is the sixth month?

_____

6 What is the last month?

_____

1st	2nd	3rd	4th	5th	6th	7th	8th	9th	10th
first	second	third	fourth	fifth	sixth	seventh	eighth	ninth	tenth

⬤ When is your birthday?

_____
_____

Let's write!

みてみて！⑪の「歯ブラシ」の「歯」はひとつひとつみがいた方がいいから、teethじゃなくてtoothなのかな…？

Words

① banana

② orange

③ pineapple

④ strawberry

⑤ watermelon

⑥ bread

⑦ egg

⑧ cake

⑨ meat

⑩ sugar

⑪ toothbrush

⑫ towel

⑬ soap

⑭ umbrella

What can I buy?

● **I have 5 dollars.**

I can buy ___two___ ___erasers___ .

I can buy ___three___ ___notebooks___ .

I can buy ___one___ ___pencil___ .

I can buy _____ _____ .

$$50¢ \times 2 = 100¢$$
$$90¢ \times 3 = 270¢$$
$$+ \ 40¢ \times 1 = \ 40¢$$
$$\overline{ 410¢}$$

Pay: 4 dollars and 10 cents

Change: 90 cents

① **I have 5 dollars.**

I can buy _____ _____ .

I can buy _____ _____ .

I can buy _____ _____ .

I can buy _____ _____ .

Pay:

Change:

② **I have 7 dollars.**

I can buy _____ _____ .

I can buy _____ _____ .

I can buy _____ _____ .

I can buy _____ _____ .

Pay:

Change:

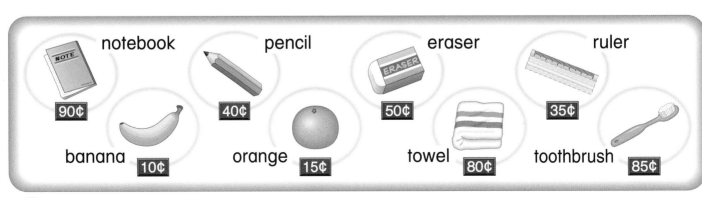

notebook 90¢   pencil 40¢   eraser 50¢   ruler 35¢

banana 10¢   orange 15¢   towel 80¢   toothbrush 85¢

Let's find words starting with each letter.

N n

O o

P p

Q q

R r

S s

T t

U u

V v

W w

X x

Y y

Z z

A B C D E F G H I J K L M N O P Q R S T U V W X Y Z

Encourage students to find words that start with each letter in their textbooks.
Pronounce each word. Ss will find that there are few words starting with X.

Supplement 1

❶ Fill in the missing letter.

① 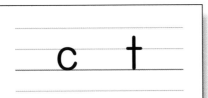 c _ t

② 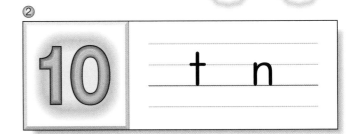 t _ n

③ 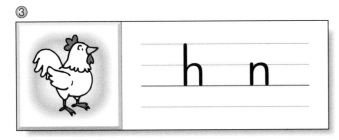 h _ n

④ 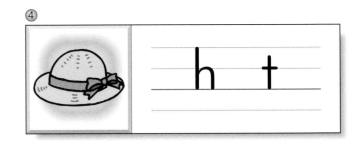 h _ t

⑤ 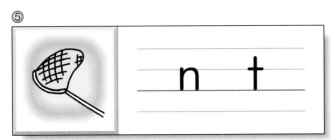 n _ t

⑥ 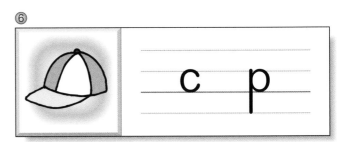 c _ p

❷ Fill in the missing letter.

① 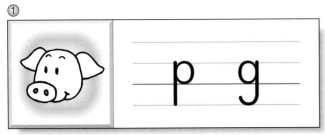 p _ g

② 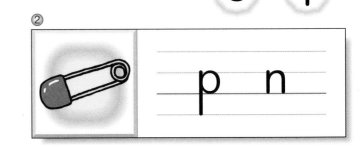 p _ n

③ 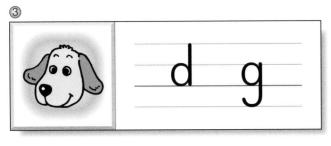 d _ g

④  f _ x

⑤ 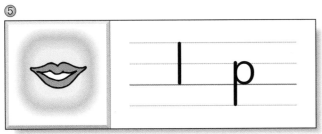 l _ p

⑥ 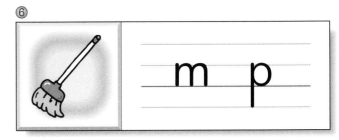 m _ p

Supplement 2

① Fill in the missing letter. a o

①  m __ p

② 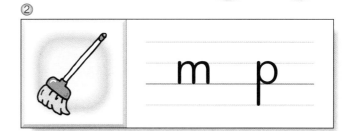 m __ p

③ 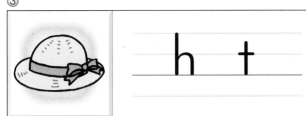 h __ t

④  f __ x

⑤ 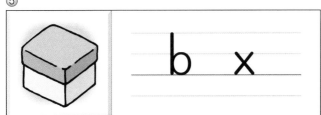 b __ x

⑥  f __ n

② Fill in the missing letter. e u

① 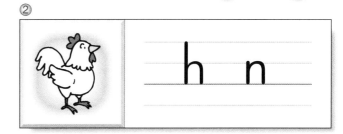 b __ d

② h __ n

③ 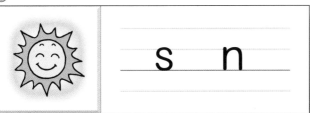 s __ n

④ c __ p

⑤ 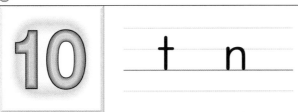 t __ n

⑥ 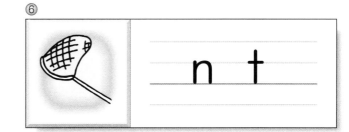 n __ t

Fill in the missing letter. ························ a e i o u

① 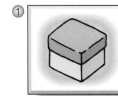 b _ x

②  m _ p

③  m _ p

④  c _ p

⑤ 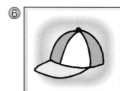 c _ t

⑥  c _ p

⑦ 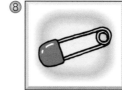 f _ x

⑧  p _ n

⑨  b _ d

⑩  d _ g

⑪  s _ n

⑫  p _ g

⑬  t _ n

⑭  l _ p

⑮  h _ n

⑯  h _ t

⑰  f _ n

⑱ _ n _ t

Supplement 4

Write the words.

① _____

② _____

③ _____

④ _____

⑤ _____

⑥ _____

⑦ _____

⑧ _____

⑨ _____

⑩ _____

⑪ _____

⑫ _____

⑬ _____

⑭ _____

⑮ _____

⑯ _____

⑰ _____

⑱ _____

Killer Whales

Killer whales live in water.

Killer whales can swim.

But they are not fish.

They are black and white.

🔵 **Fill in the blanks.**

① Killer whales live _____ .

② Killer whales can _____ .

③ They are _____ fish.

④ They are _____ and _____ .

🔵 **Answer the questions.**

① **Where** do killer whales live?

_____

② **What** can killer whales do?

_____

③ Are killer whales fish?

_____

④ **What** color are killer whales?

_____

Supplement 6

My name is Kaetlyn. My birthday is December 25th.

I like green. I like playing the piano.

I am good at skating. I want to be a piano teacher.

● Fill in the blanks.

1 My name is _____ . 2 My birthday is _____ .

3 I like _____ . 4 I like _____ .

5 I am good at _____ . 6 I want to be _____ .

● Answer the questions.

1 **What** is your name?

_____

_____

2 **When** is your birthday?

_____

_____

3 **What** color do you like?

_____

_____

4 **What** do you like to do?

_____

_____

5 **What** are you good at?

_____

_____

6 **What** do you want to be?

_____

_____